Table of Contents

Columbus, Ohio

Table of Contents

MATH

MATH GAMES AND PUZZLES

READING

In each box, draw a line from the capital letters to the small letters. The first one is done for you.

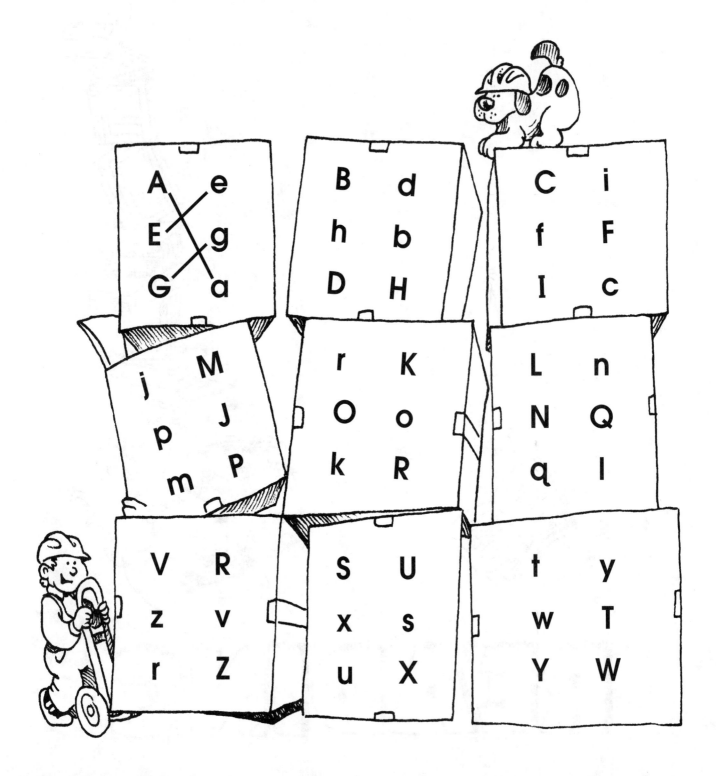

For each picture below, write the consonant it begins with on the line. The first one is done for you.

Long ā

Here is Abe's safe. It only holds things that have the **long ā** sound, such as **cape** and **game**. Look at the pictures below. Color the things that might be in the safe.

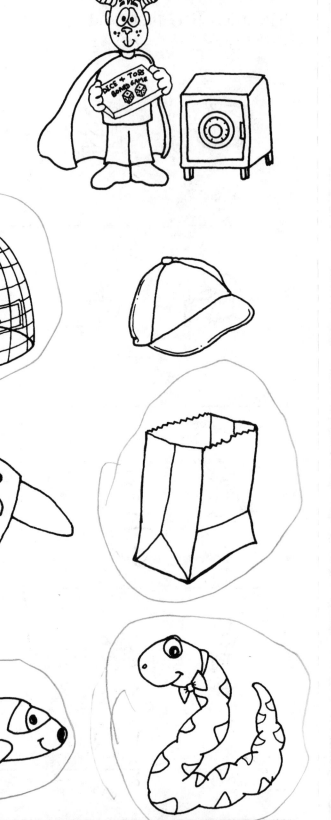

Abe wrote words that have the **long ā** sound. Draw a line from each word to its matching picture.

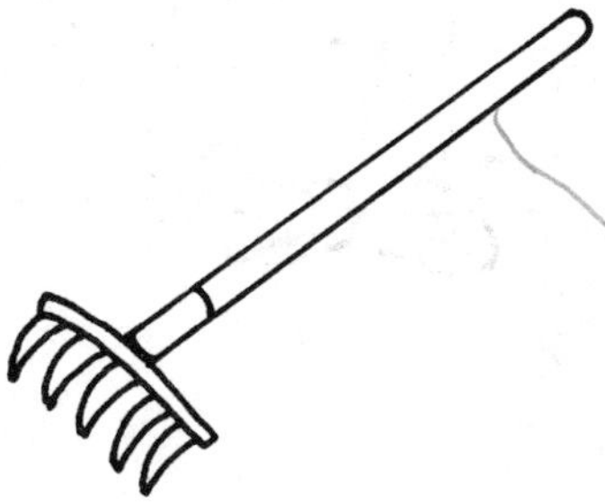

cake

cape

rake

vase

ape

plane

cave

cane

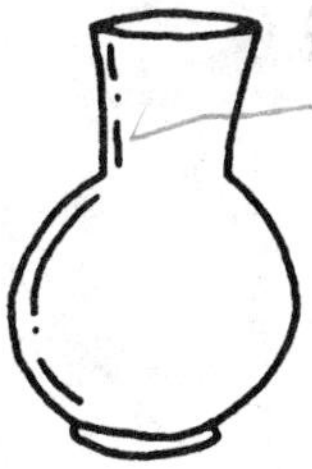

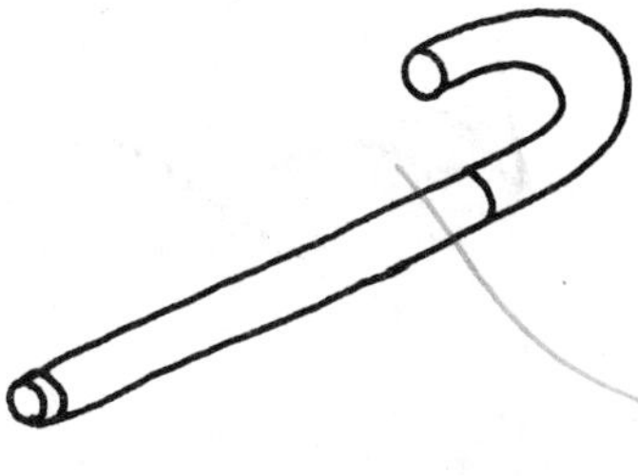

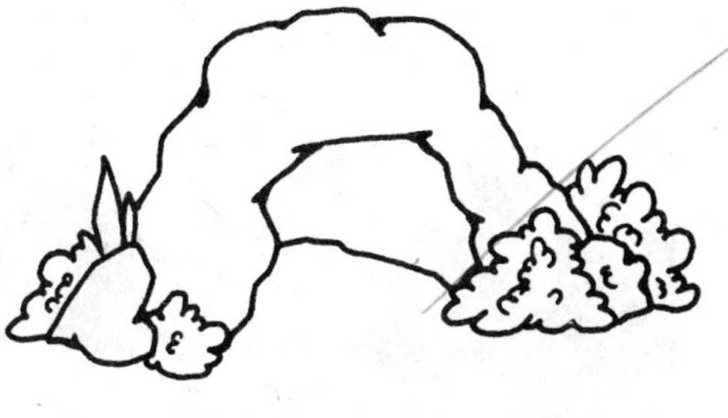

Long ā

Help the monsters get to the cave before it rains. Circle the name of each picture on the path. Then, write the names on the lines.

cane

can   cane

rake

rake   rate

tape

tap   tape

ape

ape   add

vase

vase   vine

plane

plan   plane

cage

cat   cage

Spike has many kites. Each one has a picture of something that has the **long ī** sound in its name, such as **dime**. Look at the kites below. Color the ones that belong to Spike.

Long ī

Help Spike hike down the hill. Write the word for each picture on the path. Use the words on the clouds.

pie   dime
bike   hive

fire   kite
tire   mice

kite

bike

fire

dime

mice

pie

tire

hive

Read Spike's riddles. The answer to each riddle is a **long ī** word. Write the answers on the lines. Use the words in the box.

~~nine~~	~~tire~~	~~hive~~	~~rice~~
~~pine~~	~~fire~~	~~bike~~	~~prize~~

1. This is on a car. ___tire___

2. Bees live here. ___hive___

3. This is very hot. ___fire___

4. This is a number. ___nine___

5. You can ride this. ___bike___

6. This is a tree. ___pine___

7. You can eat this. ___rice___

8. You win this. ___prize___

Find the pictures of the words you wrote. Draw a line from each word to its matching picture.

Long ō

Mo drew pictures of things around her home. **Mo** and **home** have the **long ō** sound. Color each picture that has the **long ō** sound in its name.

Help Mo get home. Color the pictures that have **long ō** in their names to make a path for her.

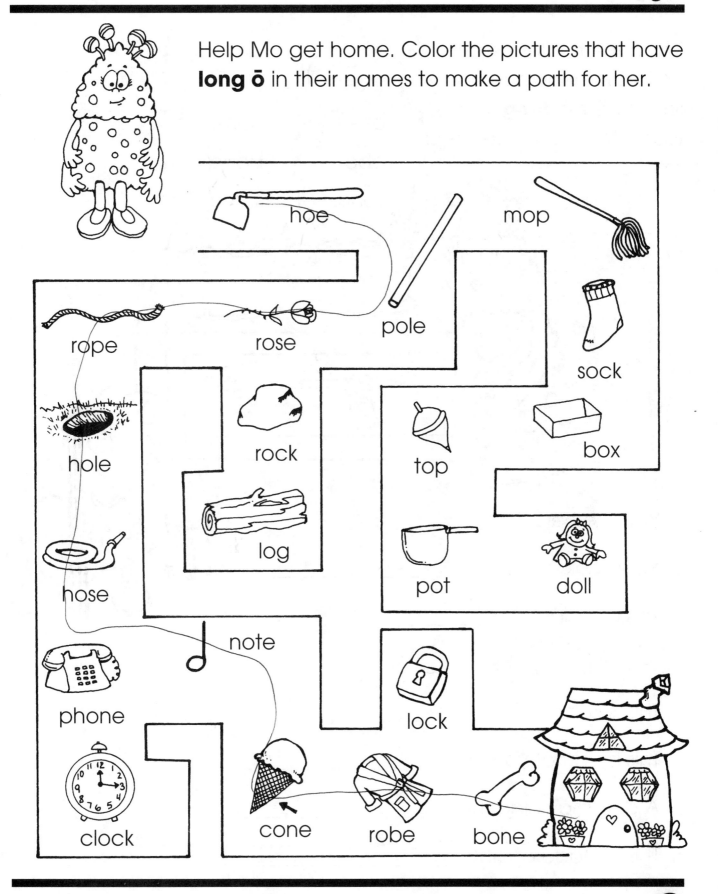

hoe

mop

pole

rope

rose

sock

hole

rock

top

box

log

hose

pot

doll

note

lock

phone

clock

cone

robe

bone

Long ō

Read the riddles below. Write the answers on the lines. Use the **long ō** words that are in the smoke.

nose
rose
robe
stone

toe
home
bone
stove

1. You live here. _____

2. You cook on this. _____

3. This is a plant. _____

4. You smell with this. _____

5. This is a rock. _____

6. This is part of your foot. _____

7. A dog may hide this. _____

8. This is made of cloth. _____

Complete the words below.
Write **a** or **o** on the lines.
Then, read the words aloud.

r_o_se   t_a_pe   b_oo_ne

c_a_ke   r_o_pe   r_a_ke

c_a_ne   v_o_se   h_o_se

p_o_le   c_a_ve   r_o_be

h_o_e   pl_a_ne   g_a_te

Long ī and ō

The monsters are going to eat
something good. To find out what it is,
color the shapes below. If a shape
has a **long ī** word in it, color it
green. If it has a **long ō** word in it,
color it blue. Color all the other
shapes yellow.

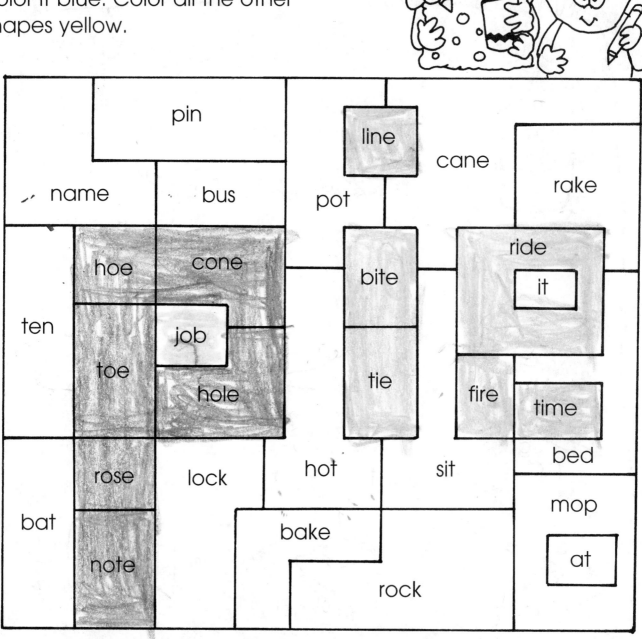

pin

line

cane

rake

name   bus   pot

hoe   cone

ride

it

ten   job   bite

toe   hole   tie   fire   time

bed

rose   lock   hot   sit

mop

bat   bake   at

note   rock

What are the monsters going to eat?_____

Lulu has a mule. The word **mule** has the **long ū** sound. Lulu's mule has a pack on his back. In it are things that have the **long ū** sound. Look at the pictures below. Color the things that might be in the pack.

glue

cup

tube

bug

cube

nut

flute

rug

duck

Long ū

Complete the sentences below with **long ū** words. Use the words in the box. Then, read the story aloud.

| mule | tune | use | flute | huge | music |

1. Lulu plays her _flute_.

2. Spike hums a _tune_.

3. Mo likes to _use_ a can for a drum.

4. Abe taps on a _huge_ box.

5. Lulu's _mule_ stamps his feet.

6. Everyone likes _music_!

Read the list below. Draw a line from each description to its matching picture.

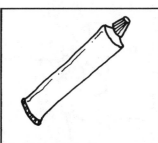

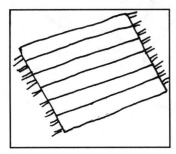

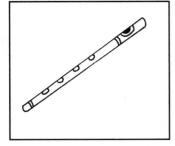

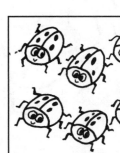

- a fine bike

- an ice cube

- a long tube

- five mice

- a huge truck

- a wide rug

- six cute bugs

- a thin flute

ai Words

Help Abe make a chain of **ai** words. Write **ai** on the lines below.
Then, say the words aloud. Listen to the **long ā** sound.

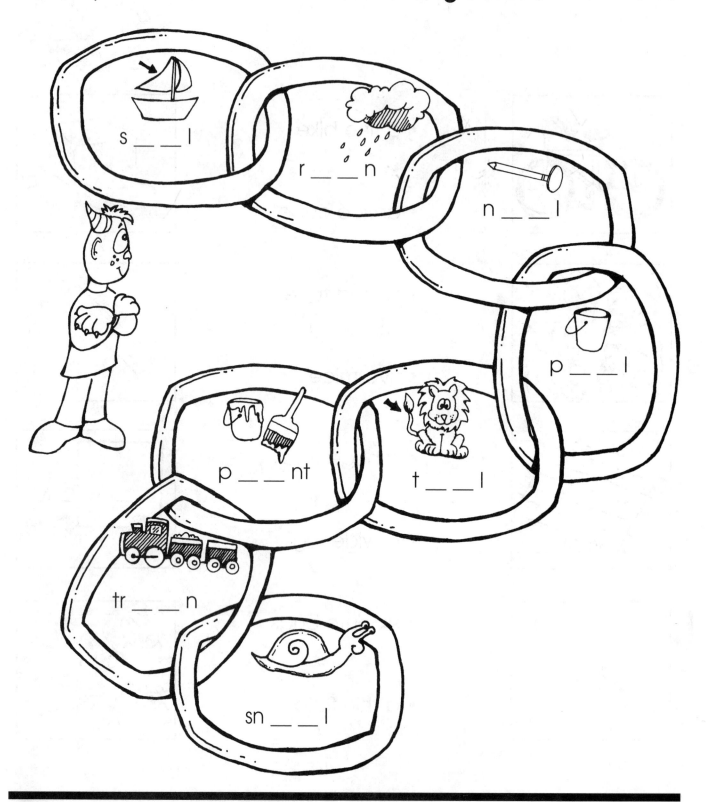

Look at the picture and the words below. Each **ay** word in the box has the **long ā** sound. Say the words aloud. Then, use the words to complete the sentences.

| day | jay | hay | stays | gray | crayons |

1. It is a rainy _____day_____.

2. Abe _____stays_____ at home.

3. He gets out a box of _____crayons_____.

4. Abe draws a _____gray_____ mule.

5. The mule is eating some _____hay_____.

6. A blue _____jay_____ is looking at the mule.

Deek made a list of **long ē** words. Each word has the letters **ee**. Read the words and write each one under the correct picture below.

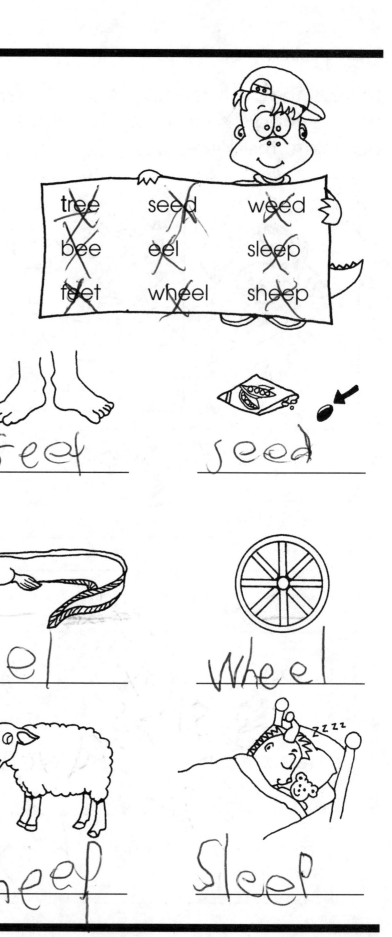

tree   seed   weed
bee   eel   sleep
feet   wheel   sheep

bee

feet

seed

tree

eel

Wheel

Weed

Sheep

Sleep

Sometimes the letters **ea** make the **long ē** sound. Write **ea** on the lines to complete the words below. Then, find the pictures of the **ea** words in the beach scene and color them.

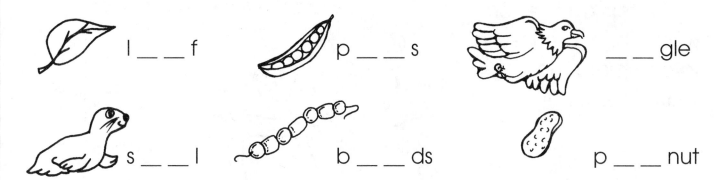

l _ _ f   p _ _ s   _ _ gle

s _ _ l   b _ _ ds   p _ _ nut

oa Words

The letters **oa** make the **long ō** sound. Read the words on Mo's boat. Circle the letters **oa** in each word. Then, use the words to complete the sentences.

coat	road	soap	roast
goat	toad	float	toast

1. A _____ has horns.

2. Mom will _____ the meat.

3. A _____ looks like a frog.

4. Mo likes to eat _____ and jam.

5. I will hang up my _____.

6. I can see six cars on the _____.

7. A boat can _____.

8. I wash my face with _____.

Help the monsters fly through the clouds. Complete the words below by writing **a**, **i**, **o** or **u** on the lines.

r___pe

k__te

g__te

t__be

f___re

c___be

h__ve

r___se

h___se

r__ke

m__le

c___ve

Long Vowels

Look at the vowel sign each monster is holding. Then, look at the snake beside the monster. Read the words on it. Color only the parts of the snake that have words with the matching vowel sound.

long ā

make
hand
rain
back
play
van

long ē

red
pea
feet
hen
seal
bee

long ī

ride
mile
pin
time
bite
pie

long ō

hot
boat
sock
hole
road
toe

long ū

sun
mule
run
cute
nut
use

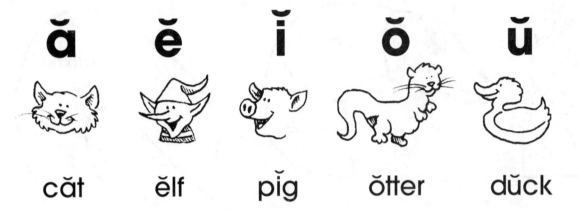

ă	ĕ	ĭ	ŏ	ŭ
căt	ĕlf	pĭg	ŏtter	dŭck

Say the name of each picture below. Write the **short vowel** you hear on the lines.

_____   _____   _____   _____   _____

_____   _____   _____   _____   _____